Ancient Egypt

LOUISE SPILSBURY

raintree
a Capstone company — publishers for children

Raintree is an imprint of Capstone Global Library Limited, a company incorporated in England and Wales having its registered office at 264 Banbury Road, Oxford, OX2 7DY – Registered company number: 6695582

www.raintree.co.uk
myorders@raintree.co.uk

Originated by Capstone Global Library Ltd
Printed and bound in India

ISBN 978 1 4747 7773 5 (hardback)
ISBN 978 1 4747 7782 7 (paperback)

British Library Cataloguing in Publication Data
A full catalogue record for this book is available from the British Library.

Acknowledgements
We would like to thank the following for permission to reproduce photographs: Cover: Shutterstock: Petr Bonek: top; Nickolay Vinokurov: bottom; Inside: Shutterstock: Anton_Ivanov: pp. 10, 22b; BasPhoto: pp. 14–15; Petr Bonek: pp. 1, 11; Ewa Studio: pp. 4–5; Irin-k: p. 15br; Sophie McAulay: pp. 36–37; Martin Mecnarowski: p. 7t; Vladimir Melnik: pp. 38–39; Mountainpix: p. 16; Orlandin: pp. 34–35; Anna Pakutina: p. 13br; Antonio Petrone: p. 41br; Evgeny Prokofyev: p. 45; R1F1: p. 28; TheRunoman: pp. 30–31; WitR: p. 35b; WitthayaP: p. 39r; Bildagentur Zoonar GmbH: p. 5br; Wikimedia Commons: p. 32; Anonymous: p. 27b; Offered by Batissier: pp. 22–23; British Museum: pp. 24–25, 26–27; Daderot: pp. 31, 33, 40–41, 42–43; Gift of Mr. and Mrs. V. Everit Macy, 1923: p. 43r; Yann Forget: pp. 20–21; Courtesy of Harrogate Museums and Arts: p. 25r; Janmad: p. 37r; Pava/JMCC1: p. 17; Rémih: pp. 12–13; Rogers Fund, 1936: p. 19r; Rogers Fund and Edward S. Harkness Gift, 1920: pp. 6–7; Maksim Sokolov (maxergon.com): p. 21br; Hedwig Storch: pp. 8–9; Aquired by Henry Walters, 1929: p. 9r; Wellcome Collection: p. 29; Charles K. Wilkinson/Rogers Fund, 1930: pp. 18–19; Yveke: p. 44.

Contents

Chapter 1 A river of life and death........................ **4**

Deadly dangers 6

Warding off evil.. 8

Chapter 2 Fearsome pharaohs........................... **10**

Cruel punishments 12

Suffering slaves.. 14

Chapter 3 Awful armies..................................... **16**

Deadly weapons 18

Vicious warriors 20

Chapter 4 Ghoulish gods................................... **22**

Power-hungry priests 24

Death and the underworld............................. 26

Chapter 5 Macabre mummies........................... **28**

Making mummies.. 30

Enclosed in coffins 32

Chapter 6 Pyramids of doom **34**

Hard labour.. 36

Chambers of secrets 38

Terrible tombs 40

Books of the Dead... 42

Doomed to die 44

Glossary... **46**

Find out more **47**

Index... **48**

CHAPTER 1

A river of life and death

Life in ancient Egypt was dangerous. People faced war, disease and starvation. In fact, for most people daily life was a battle to survive, so it is no surprise that the ancient Egyptians were obsessed with death, burials and mummies.

Egypt is a hot and dry desert country. This made it difficult for people to get enough water to drink or to grow crops. In very dry years, when little rain fell, many people starved to death.

The River Nile was precious to the ancient Egyptians. The land alongside it was one of the few places in which the soil was good enough to grow crops.

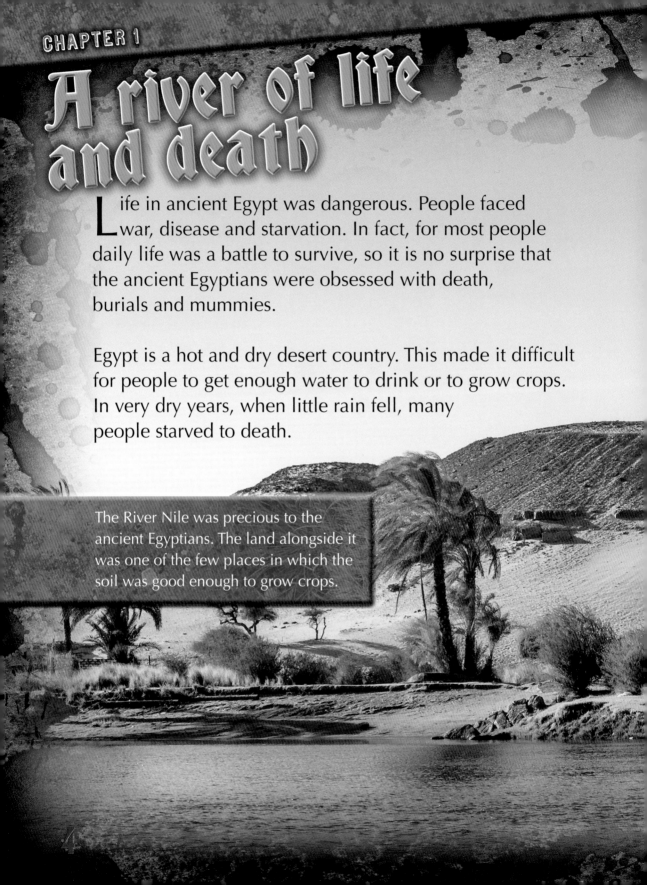

When the River Nile flooded, its mineral-rich waters covered the land alongside the river. This created rich, healthy soil in which crops could be planted. After the floods, the ancient Egyptians would give thanks to their gods. About five thousand years ago, different cities along the River Nile were brought together as one kingdom and ruled by one leader, called the pharaoh.

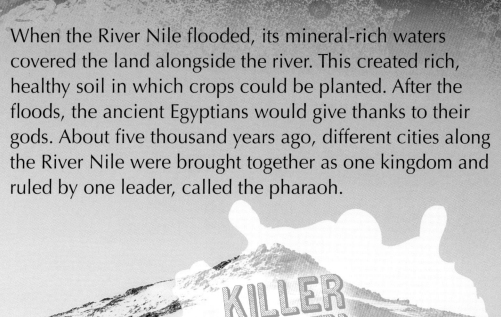

KILLER FACT!

When herding animals across flooded areas of land, many ancient Egyptians were attacked and killed by the ferocious Nile crocodiles, which lurked in the water.

The Nile crocodile was the biggest and most dangerous **predator** living in ancient Egypt.

Deadly dangers

The River Nile allowed the ancient Egyptian **civilization** to grow and to feed its people, but it also held horrible and deadly dangers.

The river allowed enemies to reach Egyptian cities and to attack them. To protect themselves, the ancient Egyptians built **fortresses** with thick, high walls, sometimes using mud from the River Nile. **Invaders** could not get into the fortresses, and the ancient Egyptians would attack them from the top of fortress towers.

Boats were used to transport everything, from people and cattle to soldiers and building blocks, up and down the Nile.

The Nile was also filled with hippopotamuses. These huge animals have powerful jaws and can be savage killers. They could **capsize** fishing boats and kill the fishermen as they fell into the river.

The hippopotamus is no longer found in Egypt, but it was once a deadly threat to boats on the River Nile.

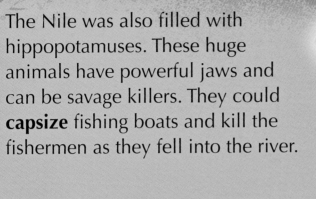

DEADLY DID YOU KNOW?

As well as hippopotamuses and crocodiles, the ancient Egyptians faced horrible attacks by other deadly wild animals. These included scorpions, fierce lions, sharp-toothed jackals and poisonous snakes.

Warding off evil

Faced with the near-constant threat of a horrible death, the ancient Egyptians wore lucky charms called amulets. They believed these could ward off evil and keep them safe. They usually wore amulets around their necks, ankles or wrists.

The ancient Egyptians wore amulets from their childhood to their death. Amulets were often placed on the chest or over the heart of a **mummy** when it was buried to protect the body and bring luck on the dead person's journey to the **afterlife**. The afterlife is the life Egyptians believed a person would live after he or she died.

ankh

This carving shows the ankh amulet. It was a popular amulet because it was the symbol for life, both on Earth and in the afterlife.

KILLER FACT!

Scarab beetles were linked to Khepri, who was believed to roll the Sun out in the morning. Scarab beetle amulets were placed in the bandages of mummies as symbols of the corpse's heart. They were also placed around the body.

The scarab beetle was the ancient Egyptian symbol for creation, so it became a popular amulet.

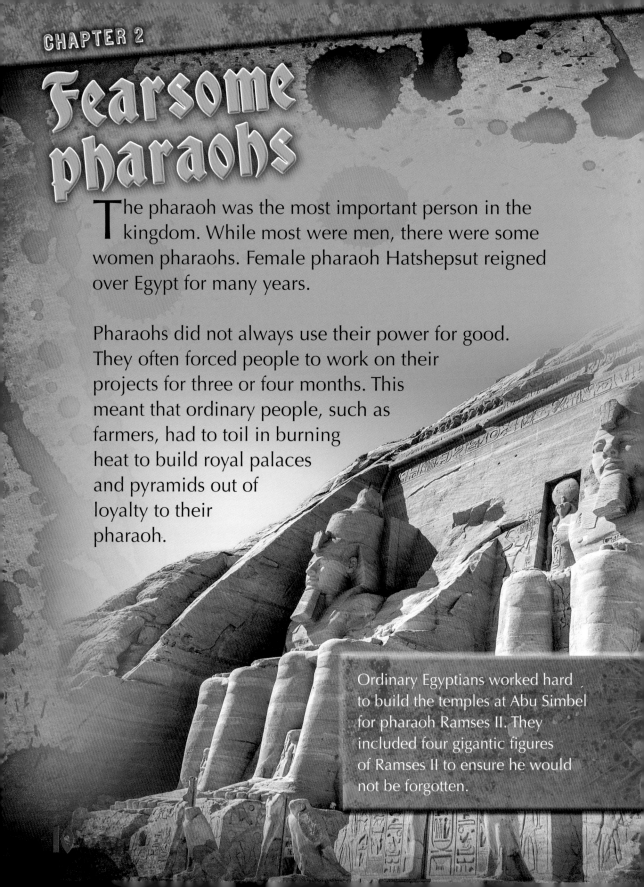

CHAPTER 2

Fearsome pharaohs

The pharaoh was the most important person in the kingdom. While most were men, there were some women pharaohs. Female pharaoh Hatshepsut reigned over Egypt for many years.

Pharaohs did not always use their power for good. They often forced people to work on their projects for three or four months. This meant that ordinary people, such as farmers, had to toil in burning heat to build royal palaces and pyramids out of loyalty to their pharaoh.

Ordinary Egyptians worked hard to build the temples at Abu Simbel for pharaoh Ramses II. They included four gigantic figures of Ramses II to ensure he would not be forgotten.

Ordinary people had to pay high **taxes** to the pharaoh. They even had to pay taxes for burying their dead relatives. These payments allowed the pharaohs to live in luxury while poor people lived in mud-brick huts. The pharaohs decorated themselves with gold and perfumes, and were not afraid of showing off the riches bought with taxpayers' money.

DEADLY DID YOU KNOW?

Tutankhamun was buried with his old sandals. The pharaoh's enemies were painted onto the soles of the sandals so that wherever he went, he trampled on his foes!

This is the pharaoh Tutankhamun's death mask, which would have been placed over his face when he died. It was made from two types of gold and decorated with gemstones.

Cruel punishments

The pharaoh had absolute power over the people and created every law. If anyone broke his rules, they could be cruelly and sometimes horribly punished.

The pharaoh's tax collectors were brutal and often punished people who missed a payment. To keep people from running away before they paid their taxes, they were thrown into deep pits or wells. If poor ordinary people owed a lot in taxes, tax collectors were allowed to torture them to death.

Egypt was known for harshly punishing captured criminals and enemies.

Some criminals had their ears and noses cut off as a warning to others not to try the same crime. A person who stole an ox could be whipped one hundred times and stabbed five times in the back. Anyone caught trying to rob a **tomb** was sentenced to death by **beheading** or drowning.

A pharaoh's crown often had a symbol of a cobra on it. This showed people that, like the cobra, he was powerful and ready to strike anyone who disobeyed him.

Pharaoh Seti I is shown here wearing a crown with a cobra.

Suffering slaves

Prisoners who had been captured in war, criminals or those who owed money were sometimes sold as **slaves**. Their owners forced them to work for nothing.

The "luckiest" slaves were put to work as servants in homes of rich Egyptians. But some slaves were forced to work long, hard hours in copper and gold mines. There, they crushed rock or burned it in fires to remove the metals, often suffering terrible injuries from their work.

These mines were also in remote places. The slaves who worked there were given little food and water, and many died after suffering from exhaustion and **dehydration**.

This stone carving shows Pharaoh Ramses II making a slave of a defeated enemy.

One pharaoh, Pepi II, had an especially cruel method of keeping insects away from himself. He ordered a slave covered in honey to stand near him. Flies swarmed all over the slave and left the pharaoh alone.

Pharaoh Pepi II hated flies, so he made a honey-covered slave stand near to him.

15

CHAPTER 3

Awful armies

The fearsome pharaohs ran an army ready to fight attacks from any invaders or enemies. The Egyptian army was one of the most feared and successful in the ancient world.

The pharaoh also used his armies for personal gain. When his army won a war, the people who had been **conquered** were forced to accept the pharaoh as their ruler. Then, they had to give the pharaoh the best and most valuable goods that they owned.

Egyptian men had to undergo tough training to become dangerous soldiers.

16

Many of the ordinary soldiers in the army were forced to be there. In wartime, they ate only what they could carry. It often took many days to reach the battlefront, so many of the soldiers were weak and hungry by the time they got there.

KILLER FACT!

Army commanders were given bronze armour for protection. Most soldiers only had light shields made from animal skins or woven papyrus to protect them against their enemies' weapons.

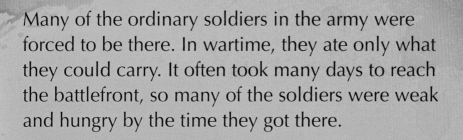

Soldiers marched long distances and into battle wearing flimsy sandals like these.

Deadly weapons

One reason the ancient Egyptian army became such a great fighting force was because of the deadly weapons its soldiers used.

Some warriors rode in horse-drawn chariots. The chariot driver wore a leather or bronze helmet and armour for protection. A soldier in the chariot fired javelins or shot arrows from a bow, which could kill enemies who were a long way away.

Foot soldiers carried a variety of dangerous weapons. These included spears, axes and short swords for cutting and stabbing. They were all used at close range while looking the enemy in the eye. The axe could be swung to slice an enemy's body into pieces.

Ancient Egyptian archers with their bows and arrows were the most-feared soldiers of all.

DEADLY DID YOU KNOW?

Soldiers were terrified of dying outside of Egypt in battle. They thought that only if they were buried near the River Nile would they have a proper funeral and be able to live on in the afterlife.

Wooden arrows could pierce the heart of an enemy when fired from a distance.

Vicious warriors

Ancient Egyptian soldiers were taught to be vicious and fierce warriors.

Soldiers were trained in wrestling, tactics and the use of weapons. They were also expected to be able to march 32 kilometres (20 miles) in one day. Discipline was strict. Soldiers were horribly beaten for the smallest mistakes to ensure they knew they had to obey orders.

The Egyptians recorded their vicious destruction of enemies in paintings such as this.

When the Egyptian army won a battle, soldiers would lift the right arm of each defeated enemy and slice off his right hand. There was a reward for each hand a soldier collected. Sometimes, these bloodthirsty prizes could be exchanged for gold.

KILLER FACT!

Daggers were used for stabbing enemies and also for slicing off their hands as trophies. This was also a good way of working out how many enemy soldiers they had killed.

The Egyptian dagger was a sharp, deadly weapon.

CHAPTER 4

Ghoulish gods

The ancient Egyptians had gods for everything, from the Sun that gave the world light and life to dangerous wild animals. They believed that their gods would protect them from terrible dangers, as long as they worshipped the gods properly and kept them happy.

Some gods looked like human beings, but others were scary-looking creatures that were part human and part animal. For example, Sekhmet was the fierce goddess of war and battle, so she had the head of a lioness. The Sun god Ra appeared as a man with the head of a hawk.

Ra was the most important god of the ancient Egyptians. They believed Ra died at the end of each day and sailed through the **underworld** until dawn.

Some of the gods looked gruesome, but the ancient Egyptians also found them comforting. They believed that by making dangerous animals such as lions into gods, the animals were less likely to attack them.

KILLER FACT!

Sobek was one of the scariest looking gods. He was the god of the crocodiles, which the ancient Egyptians feared. Some temples to Sobek kept live crocodiles, which people could worship.

As crocodiles were ferocious and strong, Sobek was the god of the Egyptian army.

Power-hungry priests

The ancient Egyptians respected and feared their gods, so the priests who carried out **rituals** to please the gods were very powerful. People were often afraid of the priests.

The priests prepared dead bodies for the afterlife. While making mummies, they often wore a mask of the god Anubis to strike fear into the hearts of the people. Anubis was the god of **embalming** and he had the ghoulish head of a jackal. Priests must have looked terrifying during this ceremony.

This painting shows a priest wearing an Anubis mask as he performs rituals.

To enable the dead person to see, smell, breathe, hear and eat in the afterlife, the priest would perform the Opening of the Mouth ceremony. The priest would touch the mouth and face of the mummy, read out spells and, sometimes, **sacrifice** a calf.

DEADLY DID YOU KNOW?

The god Anubis had the head of a jackal because these wild animals were often seen around the edges of the desert, near to where the dead were buried.

The ancient Egyptians gave Anubis the head of a jackal because they thought jackals watched over people in the afterlife.

Death and the underworld

The ancient Egyptians believed that people went to the underworld after they died. There, the gods decided what happened to a dead person in the afterlife by testing their heart.

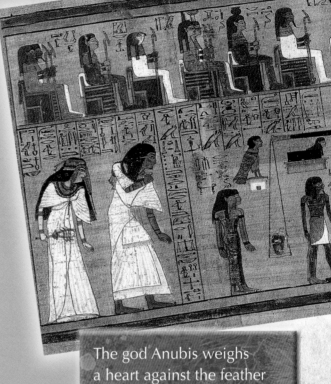

The god Anubis weighs a heart against the feather of the goddess Maat to test if the person was good.

The heart of a dead person was weighed to find out if he or she had lived a good life. If the heart passed the test, the person could spend his or her afterlife in a heavenly paradise. Here, he or she would live the same way as on Earth. For example, a pharaoh would still be a pharaoh and a farmer would still be a farmer.

If a person had been bad and his or her heart failed the test, it was fed to Ammit. The name Ammit means "devourer". Ammit was the scary female demon-goddess of the underworld.

KILLER FACT!

Ammit was part lion, hippopotamus and crocodile – a horrible and terrifying combination of the three largest and most feared animals in the ancient Egyptian world.

When Ammit ate a person's heart, this was the end of his or her afterlife.

CHAPTER 5

Macabre mummies

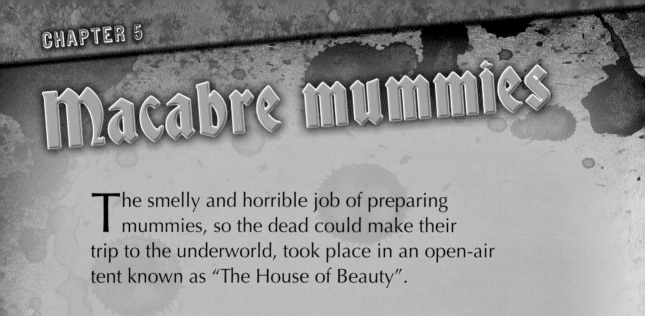

The smelly and horrible job of preparing mummies, so the dead could make their trip to the underworld, took place in an open-air tent known as "The House of Beauty".

First, the dead body was carefully cleaned. Then the embalmers sliced it open to take out body parts such as the liver and stomach with their bare hands. They left the heart inside.

The grisly job of making a mummy took up to seventy days altogether.

Next, the body was covered in a kind of salt to dry it out. After forty days, the salt was removed and the body was oiled to keep the skin from cracking. As the body dried out, it lost shape, so rags and straw were stuffed inside it to give it a lifelike shape again. Sometimes, false eyes were added, too.

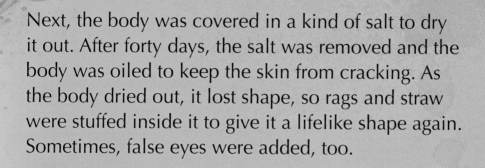

KILLER FACT!

To remove the brain, a long, slightly hooked tool was pushed up the nose into the skull and swirled round to turn the brain to liquid. This mush then dripped out through the nose.

Ancient Egyptians often used the same knives for **mummification** as they did for preparing and eating meat!

29

Making mummies

After the body was dried out, it would not decay, but it was not a pretty sight. It would have shrivelled up and the skin would have darkened. This gruesome **corpse** was then wrapped up in fine linen cloth.

It took about fifteen days to wrap the body in the linen cloth. It was a delicate job because the body was quite fragile. If a priest snapped off a finger or toe while wrapping it, he replaced it with a piece of wood and covered it quickly with a bandage.

At different stages, the linen strips were painted with warm **resin**. This helped stick the bandages together. While the mummy was being wrapped, a priest read out spells to help the dead person go safely to the underworld.

If the bandages of an ancient Egyptian mummy were unwrapped, they would be 1.6 kilometres (1 mile) long.

KILLER FACT!

The liver, lungs, intestines and stomach were mummified separately. A worker, called the pickler, stored these body parts in four special pots called canopic jars.

Ancient Egyptians believed that the body parts stored in the canopic jars would be needed in the afterlife.

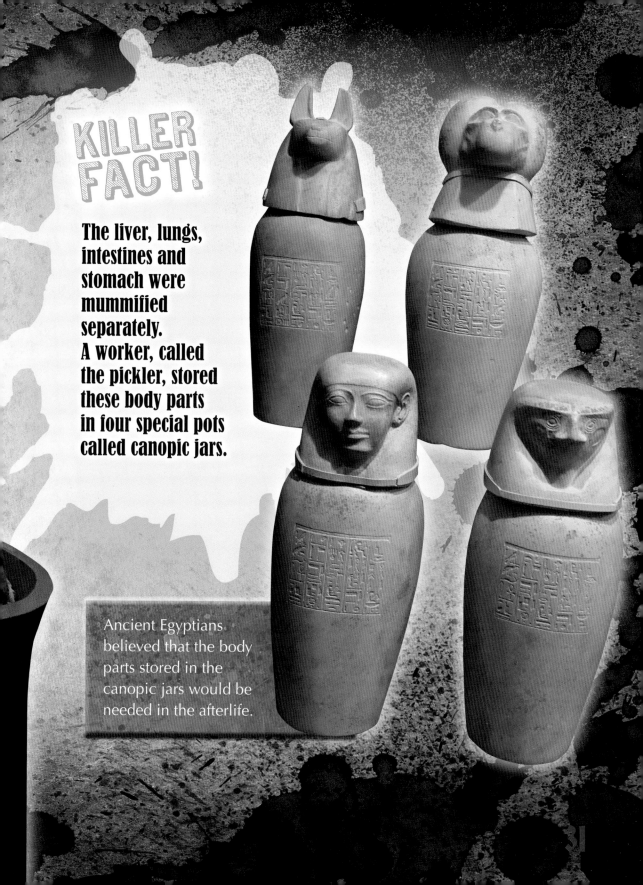

31

Enclosed in coffins

Being made into a mummy was an expensive process, so it was mostly pharaohs and other rich people who were mummified. Once a mummy was complete, it was enclosed in a coffin.

Some Egyptian mummies were buried in two or three different coffins, nested one inside the other. One reason for these containers was to protect the body from being taken by wild animals or tomb robbers.

Tutankhamun's body was buried in three coffins nested within each other. The innermost one was made of solid gold.

The outer coffin was sometimes a s[...]
called a **sarcophagus**. A sarcopha[gus...]
usually displayed above ground, a[nd...]
decorated. Some were even mad[e...]
When the mummy was safely en[...]
coffins, it was placed inside a p[...]

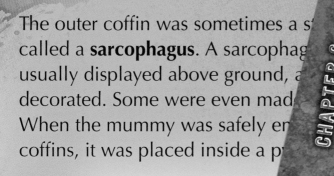

DEADLY DID YOU KNOW?

Some coffins were shaped like a mummy's body and eerily decorated with a face and wig to look like the dead person. If the body was lost or destroyed, the coffin became a substitute so that person could still have an afterlife.

Coffins were decorated with protective spells and maps that showed the route to the afterlife.

33

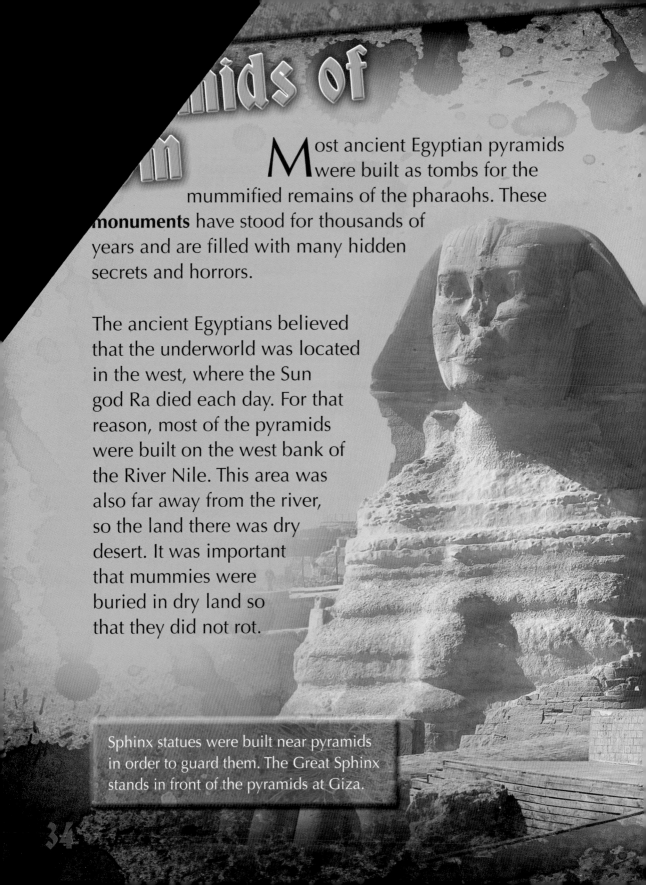

Most ancient Egyptian pyramids were built as tombs for the mummified remains of the pharaohs. These **monuments** have stood for thousands of years and are filled with many hidden secrets and horrors.

The ancient Egyptians believed that the underworld was located in the west, where the Sun god Ra died each day. For that reason, most of the pyramids were built on the west bank of the River Nile. This area was also far away from the river, so the land there was dry desert. It was important that mummies were buried in dry land so that they did not rot.

Sphinx statues were built near pyramids in order to guard them. The Great Sphinx stands in front of the pyramids at Giza.

The sphinxes that guarded the pyramids had the body of a lion and the head of a pharaoh or a god. Sphinxes were often huge. The Great Sphinx, for example, is 73 metres (240 feet) long and 20 metres (66 feet) high. Some sphinxes were painted in bold colours to terrify passersby.

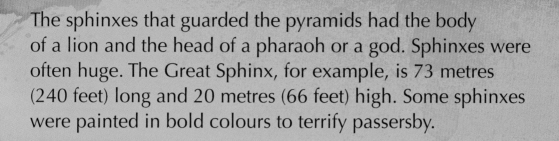

DEADLY DID YOU KNOW?

When a pharaoh died, his or her mummy was prepared for its tomb immediately. When a queen died, her body was left to decay for three or four days before it was mummified.

These are the pyramids at Giza. The smaller pyramids in the foreground were built for dead queens.

Hard labour

The towering pyramids were built next to the River Nile so that stone blocks could be brought to the building site by boat. These mighty monuments were huge, and building them was hot and exhausting work.

We do not know for certain how the pyramids were built, but the Egyptians probably created a sloping ramp of brick, earth and sand around the base. Workers most likely hauled stone blocks up the ramp using sledges, rollers and levers. They made the ramp higher and longer as the pyramid became taller and wider.

Pyramids were once covered with glistening white limestone, but that was stolen long ago.

The Great Pyramid is the largest and most famous of the ancient Egyptian pyramids. It is more than 140 metres (460 feet) high and took more than twenty years to build, during which time workers had to move 2,300,000 building blocks, weighing about 2.2 tonnes each.

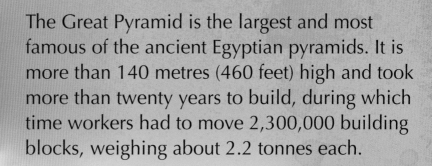

DEADLY DID YOU KNOW?
The ancient Egyptians spent much of their lives thinking about and planning for their deaths. Some pharaohs even started building their tombs as soon as they came to power.

Scribes were men who could read and write in ancient Egypt. They kept accounts and ordered supplies for pyramid builders.

Chambers of secrets

Pyramids were designed to protect a pharaoh's body and his precious belongings. The builders knew that grave robbers would try to break in to pyramids to steal the treasure inside, so they built them with clever obstacles and traps!

If would-be robbers managed to get inside a pyramid, they faced the challenge of mazes, confusing passageways, sliding doors, trapdoors, and secret doorways and chambers.

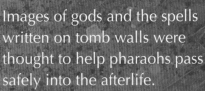

Images of gods and the spells written on tomb walls were thought to help pharaohs pass safely into the afterlife.

The pharaoh was buried in a room in the darkest, deepest depths of the pyramid to try to hide his tomb from raiders. To help protect the pharaoh and his treasures, walls of the inner tomb were painted with spells.

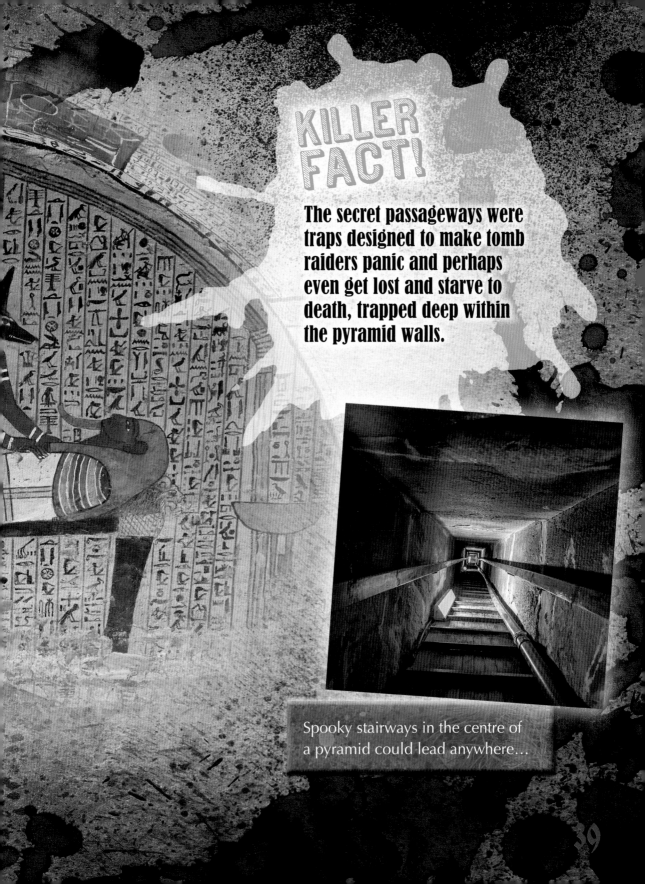

KILLER FACT!

The secret passageways were traps designed to make tomb raiders panic and perhaps even get lost and starve to death, trapped deep within the pyramid walls.

Spooky stairways in the centre of a pyramid could lead anywhere...

Terrible tombs

The secret tomb hidden within the depths of a pyramid was deathly dark and quiet. It was filled with a strange, and sometimes terrible, selection of objects.

The ancient Egyptians put everything in the tomb they thought a pharaoh would need in the afterlife. This included things such as jewellery, clothes, furniture and even a toilet. The ancient Egyptians believed these objects would be magically transported to the underworld with the pharaoh.

Model boats like the one in this photograph were put in tombs so pharaohs could travel in the afterlife.

Early pharaohs were buried with their real servants. These unfortunate workers were killed and buried with their masters to serve him in the afterlife. Later, pharaohs were a bit kinder and were buried with models of their servants, instead.

KILLER FACT!

A pharaoh's pet cats often had their necks broken and were then mummified and buried alongside the pharaoh to keep him company in the afterlife.

Sometimes, cats were mummified as offerings to the gods.

Books of the Dead

A scary-sounding Book of the Dead was usually buried deep inside a pyramid alongside the mummy's coffin. These terrible tomes were intended to help the dead person survive the afterlife.

A Book of the Dead was like a manual or guidebook to the afterlife. It included spells and passwords. It also told the dead person things they needed to know, such as where to go, how to speak to different gods and what to say at certain times.

Without a Book of the Dead, ancient Egyptians feared they would suffer a fate worse than death in the underworld.

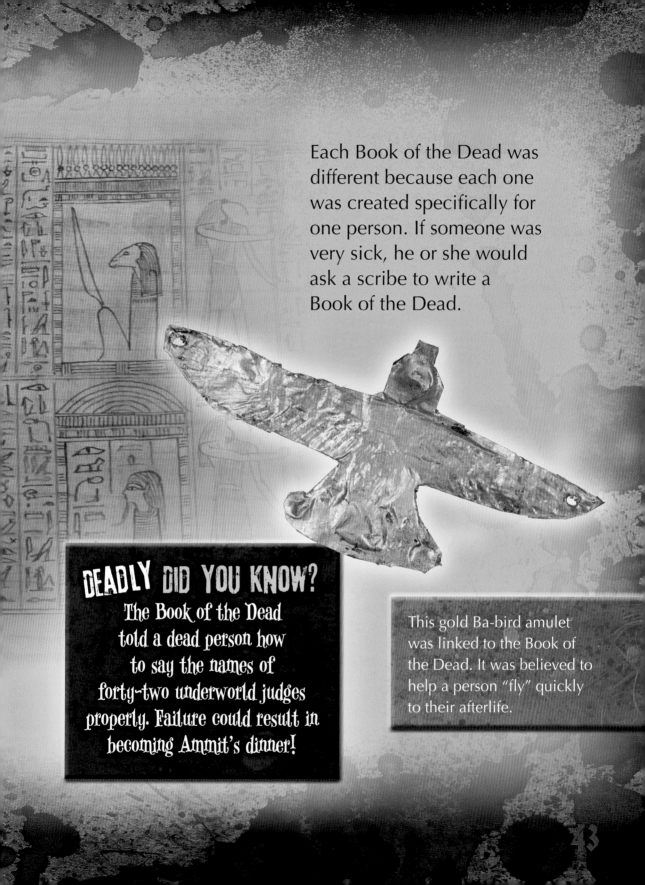

Each Book of the Dead was different because each one was created specifically for one person. If someone was very sick, he or she would ask a scribe to write a Book of the Dead.

DEADLY DID YOU KNOW?
The Book of the Dead told a dead person how to say the names of forty-two underworld judges properly. Failure could result in becoming Ammit's dinner!

This gold Ba-bird amulet was linked to the Book of the Dead. It was believed to help a person "fly" quickly to their afterlife.

Doomed to die

The mysterious **hieroglyphs** written on walls, coffins and Books of the Dead made some people believe the pyramids were **cursed** and that the people who entered them were doomed to die.

Archaeologist Howard Carter and his team found the tomb of Tutankhamun and removed its treasures in 1922. Within a short time, members of the team became sick and some even died. Some people believed this was all because of the curse of Tutankhamun's mummy.

Did opening Tutankhamun's tomb and removing treasures such as this throne unleash a terrible curse?

Like the pharaohs, the great civilization of ancient Egypt was doomed to die, too. Periods of bad weather ruined crops, and many Egyptians starved. The pharaohs also did not keep their armies well-supplied, so when enemies invaded, the armies could not fight. When Alexander the Great conquered Egypt in 332 BC, the ancient Egyptian way of life ended.

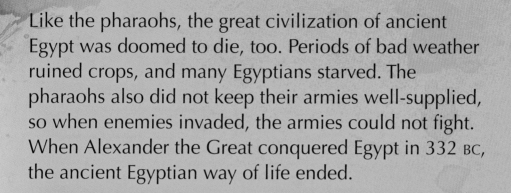

KILLER FACT!

Few people believe in the mummy's curse today, but tomb builders in ancient Egypt probably used the threat to make people too terrified to go into the pyramids.

The pyramid tombs were built to last. They are important remains of ancient Egyptian life.

Glossary

afterlife life after death. Some people believe that after we die we go to live in another world.

archaeologist person who studies objects to learn about how people lived in the past

beheading cutting off a person's head to kill him or her

capsize when a boat turns upside down in water

civilization settled community in which people live together and use systems such as writing to communicate

conquered used force to take over a city or country

corpse dead body

cursed being under a curse – words said so that harm comes to someone

dehydration lack of water

embalming treating a dead body in order to stop it decaying

fortresses large, strong buildings that can be defended from attack

hieroglyphs symbols that represent words, parts of words or sounds

invaders people, armies or countries that use force to enter and take control of another country.

monuments statues, buildings or other structures made to remember an event, time or person

mummification way to preserve a dead body by treating it with oils and wrapping it in strips of cloth

mummy dead body that has been preserved and wrapped in bandages

papyrus tall grass-like plant that grows in marshes

predator animal that kills other animals for food

resin sticky substance that comes from trees

rituals ceremonies performed for religious reasons

sacrifice kill an animal or human to honour a god or gods

sarcophagus stone coffin

scribe person in ancient Egypt trained to read and write hieroglyphs

slaves people who are owned by other people and have to obey them

taxes money paid to a ruler or government

tomb building where dead people are laid to rest

underworld mythical world of the dead

Find out more

Books

Ancient Egypt (History Hunters), Nancy Dickmann (Raintree, 2016)

Daily Life in Ancient Egypt (Daily Life in Ancient Civilizations), Don Nardo (Raintree, 2016)

DKfindout! Ancient Egypt, DK (DK Children, 2017)

Egyptian Myths and Legends (All About Myths), Fiona Macdonald (Raintree, 2013)

Geography Matters in Ancient Egypt, Melanie Waldron (Raintree, 2015)

Websites

www.bbc.com/bitesize/topics/zg87xnb/resources/2
Watch these videos to learn more about ancient Egypt.

www.dkfindout.com/uk/history/ancient-egypt
Find out more about ancient Egypt, and take a quiz to test your knowledge.

Index

afterlife 8, 19, 24, 25, 26, 33,
   40, 41, 42
Ammit 26, 27, 43
amulets 8, 9
armour 17, 18
army 16–17, 18, 20, 45

beheading 12
boats 7, 36
Book of the Dead 42–43

canopic jars 31
cats 41
chariots 18
coffins 32–33, 42, 44
crocodiles 5, 7, 23, 27

fortresses 6

gods and goddesses 5, 10,
   22–23, 24, 25, 26, 34, 35, 42

hieroglyphs 44
hippopotamuses 7, 27

mines 14
mummies 4, 8, 9, 24, 25,
   28–29, 30–31, 32–33, 34, 35,
   41, 42, 44, 45

Nile, River 5, 6–7, 19, 34, 36

pharaohs 5, 10–11, 12, 13, 15,
   16, 26, 32, 34, 35, 37, 38,
   40, 41, 45
priests 24–25, 30
punishments 12–13
pyramids 10, 33, 34–35,
   36–37, 38–39, 40, 42, 44, 45

robbers 12, 32, 38

sarcophagus 33
scarab beetles 9
scribes 37, 43
slaves 14–15
soldiers 17, 18, 19, 20, 21
sphinxes 35
symbols 9, 13

taxes 11, 12
tomb 12, 32, 33, 34, 35, 37,
   38, 39, 40–41, 44, 45
torture 12
Tutankhamun 9, 44

underworld 22, 26, 28, 30, 34,
   40, 43

weapons 17, 18–19, 20–21
wild animals 7, 22, 25, 32